Mystery at Ardfuar

and other stories for girls

Ruth Burke

© Day One Publications 2007
First printed 2007

ISBN 978-1-84625-069-9

9 781846 250699 >

All Scripture quotations in chapter one are from the
Authorised Version Crown Copyright, all other quotations, are taken from
the **New International Version**®. Copyright © 1973,1978,1984
Used by permission. All rights reserved.
British Library Cataloguing in Publication Data available

Published by Day One Publications
Ryelands Road, Leominster, HR6 8NZ
☎ 01568 613 740 FAX 01568 611 473
email—sales@dayone.co.uk
web site—www.dayone.co.uk
North American—e-mail—sales@dayonebookstore.com
North American—web site—www.dayonebookstore.com

Illustrations by Bradley Goodwin
Designed by Bradley Goodwin and printed by Gutenberg Press, Malta

Contents

To Gareth
with love and thanks for your encouragement

Aunt Roberta's secrets

'Oh, yes, I nearly forgot. Can you come with me on Saturday to ask Aunt Roberta to bake me a birthday cake?' asked Lisa, zipping up her jacket.

'Come on, girls, hurry up. You two are the last out of here every afternoon,' called Mrs Morris from the cloakroom door.

Lisa and Amy picked up their bags and hurried outside. The playground was nearly empty.

'Who's Aunt Roberta and why does she make your birthday cake?' asked Amy.

Lisa shrugged. 'I'm not sure who she is exactly. Mum's aunt, I think. She was a missionary somewhere. She's ancient, but she still bakes fantastic cakes. She has no phone, so we'll have to go to her house. Dad's away, but Mum said I could go on the bus, if you were allowed to come with me.'

Amy was sure she would be allowed. They were nearly always together on Saturdays. Lisa had no brothers or sisters, so she often joined in with what Amy and Mark were doing. They saw each other on Sundays too, since they went to the same church. The 'ancient' Aunt Roberta sounded rather interesting—as long as Lisa was there to talk to her.

Aunt Roberta's house turned out to be right on

the other side of town. Amy had never been so far on the bus before. The girls jumped off at the terminus and found themselves in a sprawling estate of grey houses with big gardens but few flowers. Lisa's mum had drawn them a map, so that they would be sure to find Aunt Roberta's house. 'This is it,' Lisa announced. 'I recognize the curtains.'

She rang the doorbell, then gave one of her giggles and dived round the side of the house. Amy groaned to herself. This was Lisa's idea of a joke. Aunt Roberta would come to the door and have no idea who Amy was. Amy would be so embarrassed, and Lisa would enjoy it all enormously.

Aunt Roberta took forever to answer the door. Amy was about to leave the doorstep and drag Lisa back, when there was a rattle and the door opened a crack. Aunt Roberta did look old. She was very small and very thin. Her white hair was pulled back from her face into a bun, and the face looked puzzled. Amy smiled foolishly and tried to think of something to say. Just then Lisa came round the corner, laughing. Aunt Roberta's face relaxed into a smile, and she opened the door wide for the girls to go inside.

While Lisa explained about the cake, Amy studied Aunt Roberta and her living room. They were both clean and tidy, but a little shabby. The curtains looked even uglier from inside. Aunt Roberta offered them a drink of milk and brought some biscuits. She watched while they ate, obviously delighted with her visitors.

'Have another biscuit,' she urged, but Lisa shook her head politely and screwed up her nose at Amy behind Aunt Roberta's back. Amy took one, even though they were soft. The poor old lady had probably baked them weeks ago and kept them in a tin in the hope that someone might call.

When Lisa's mum went to collect the cake and saw how frail Aunt Roberta had become over the last few months, she decided that she ought to be visiting her more often.

Sometimes she sent Lisa and Amy on their own.

'We've lots of other things to do,' moaned Lisa, but they actually rather enjoyed the visits. In fact, it worked out very well, because their class began to do a history project and they were supposed to interview elderly members of their families. Aunt Roberta told them lots of stories about her childhood as the eldest of nine brothers and sisters and about her time in Brazil, where she had seen many exciting things happen in the church. Lisa and Amy were fascinated and chose some stories to write up for their project.

By now Lisa felt quite at home with Aunt Roberta, so one Saturday afternoon she plunged right in: 'Some people in our class have been bringing in interesting objects from the past. We were wondering if you had anything we could borrow.'

Amy looked around the room. There was very little in it. A solitary clock stood on the mantelpiece and even the china cabinet was almost empty.

'Well,' said Aunt Roberta. 'I'd love to help, but, you see, I've given most of my things away already. I'm all packed up and ready to go.'

'Go where?' asked Lisa.

Aunt Roberta looked surprised. 'Heaven, of course,' she said.

Amy stared at her. Did Aunt Roberta think about heaven all the time? Only last week she had heard her tell Lisa's mum not to worry about getting her any clothes, because she had enough to last her till she got to heaven! Amy sometimes thought about heaven, but not often, because it involved thinking about dying, and that was just too scary.

On the bus on the way home Lisa couldn't stop talking about the ruby ring Aunt Roberta was going to lend them. Amy had missed that.

'Didn't you hear her say she has a ring we can borrow for our project? You'd never think she had a valuable ring hidden away. Nobody else will bring anything as good as that. Maybe John will stop boasting about his gas mask. I'm fed up hearing about his granddad and the air raids.'

Amy looked out of the window and thought about the ring. It was an engagement ring, of course. Somewhere in the past there had been a handsome young man. But the beautiful, young Roberta had had to leave him behind when she sailed for Brazil …

Lisa's mum was sceptical when she heard the theory. 'I must say I never heard of a romance in Aunt Roberta's life. The only ring I know about is that signet ring she always wears. But if she does lend you a ring you must take good care of it.'

She insisted on coming with them to collect it. After tea Aunt Roberta got up stiffly from her armchair and went into the kitchen. She came back carrying a round cake tin. Putting it down on the coffee table, she opened the lid. Inside was a cake with a hole in the middle, like a huge doughnut, beautifully decorated with chocolate curls and sugar flowers. It smelt delicious.

'There you are,' said Aunt Roberta with a touch

of pride, '"Ruby's Ring." It's a long time since I baked that cake. I used to make it for all my brothers and sisters on their birthdays. To think I'm the only one left of them all. It's a long time since anyone called me "Ruby" either.'

The girls' mouths dropped open. Mum looked as if she was going to laugh out loud, but she managed not to, until they were in the car on their way home.

'How are you going to explain that one to the rest of the class?' she asked.

Lisa just shrugged. 'Oh, well, I'm sure everyone would far rather have a slice of cake than see some old ring anyway. And if John says one word, he'll just not get any.'

But Amy was terribly disappointed. She had woven a romantic story around Aunt Roberta, and now it had disappeared with the ring.

Not long afterwards, something much more upsetting happened. Without any warning, Lisa announced that her family was moving away. Amy couldn't believe it. Why? Where? When?

Lisa could hardly believe it herself. 'You know my dad's been having to work away from home a lot. He wanted a job where he wouldn't have to travel so much, and now he's found one in some hole-in-the-hedge place called Eldershore. It's hundreds of miles from here, and I don't know a single soul. I'm just not going!'

But she had no choice. One weekend she went with her parents to visit Eldershore and came back quite excited.

'Our new house is huge and it's only five minutes from the beach,' she reported, but Amy didn't want to hear about it. It would be fine for Lisa; she would make hundreds of new friends. When they met up again at church camp the next summer it would be as if they had never known each other. And what was she supposed to do? She couldn't imagine life without Lisa.

Lisa decided to solve that problem before she left. Laura had no particular friend in the class. Perhaps she would like to team up with Amy.

'Maybe,' said Laura, 'but she's too quiet and I'm not sure we like the same sort of things.'

Amy wasn't meant to hear, but she did, and it wasn't a very good start. At least she would have a partner when Mrs Morris shouted, 'Get into twos!'

And what was to become of Aunt Roberta? 'Once we've gone you'll have to visit her,' decreed Lisa. 'She has no other relatives left here.'

Since she found herself with plenty of spare time on her hands once Lisa had left, Amy did go to see

Aunt Roberta fairly often. One Saturday morning Aunt Roberta showed her how to make 'Ruby's Ring.' Amy had noticed that the old lady was becoming very wobbly, so she wasn't too surprised to come home from school one afternoon to the news that Aunt Roberta had had a fall and was in hospital.

'Lisa's mum rang me,' explained Mum, 'and asked me to go and see her. I'd like you to come with me. Sometimes when older people have a fall it can make them a bit confused and it might help to see a familiar face.'

Amy remembered the last time she had had to go to a hospital. Mark had broken his wrist and she had had to sit with him for hours in Accident and Emergency. But she wanted to see that Aunt Roberta was all right, so she didn't object to going with Mum, even though they probably wouldn't be back in time for Youth Group.

It took ages to find Aunt Roberta's bed, and when they did find it, Amy thought at first that there was some mistake. Aunt Roberta didn't look at all like herself. Her white hair was combed out loose over the pillow and she had a nasty bruise above one eye. In her nightie she looked even thinner, and her skin hung in folds as if it was too big for her arms. Someone had taped her ring to her finger so that it wouldn't slip off. She spoke very little that first evening, but she certainly knew Amy and smiled at her a lot. Mum held her hand and said soothing things. Just as they were about to leave, Aunt Roberta asked Mum to read, and motioned to the Bible on her locker. Mum opened it and gave Amy a look which meant, 'How can anyone see this print?'

She read from Isaiah 43

Fear not: for I have redeemed thee, I have called thee by thy name; thou art mine. When thou passest through the waters, I will be with thee; and through the rivers, they shall not overflow thee …

Aunt Roberta repeated the words along with her.

'Maybe she doesn't need to worry about the tiny print because she knows the whole Bible by heart,' thought Amy.

When she wrote to Lisa she gave a full account of Aunt Roberta's accident, but told her not to worry.

'My family can visit,' she wrote. 'Even Mark doesn't mind going to see her. She never complains about the food or the nurses like some of the other old ladies do. I think she's enjoying having so many people to tell her stories to.'

Lisa's letters to Amy were not nearly as cheerful as Amy had expected. There wasn't much to do in Eldershore. The church was small and there was noone Lisa's age there. None of the girls at school were anywhere near as nice as Amy. There were two pieces of good news. At last she had persuaded her parents to allow her to have a dog. And it was only 173 days until camp! She usually added at least one postscript. The latest letter had two:

P.S. Don't forget to write back SOON!

P.P.S. MIZPAH.

Amy sat looking at the blue page. She was glad that she was still Lisa's best friend, but she didn't want her to be so terribly miserable. And what was 'MIZPAH' supposed to mean? Was it some kind of code? For a few days she puzzled over it, but was none the wiser. She didn't want to ask anyone else for help in case it was a secret. Perhaps Lisa would send another clue.

To her surprise, Amy came across the next clue one Sunday morning in church. The minister was talking about Saul becoming king and how Samuel had gathered the people together at Mizpah. Mizpah! Amy plucked Mark's Bible out of his hands. He scowled at her, but there wasn't much more he could do, sitting in church with his father beside him. Mark's Bible had maps at the back. Amy found out where Mizpah was and that the name meant 'Watchtower.' Disappointed, she handed Mark back his Bible. It wasn't much of a clue after all. What was Lisa on about?

Aunt Roberta had broken her arm in the fall, and, as it was taking a long time to heal, she had to stay in hospital for several weeks. At first Amy had been shy about going on her own to visit. She found it awkward dealing with some of the other patients and she was scared of one of the nurses too: she always seemed to be cross. Going on her own did mean that Amy got a chance to talk to Aunt Roberta, though. That didn't happen if there were other adults there. Everyone was fascinated by her stories and everyone came away knowing that Aunt Roberta's own favourites were the ones that ended with someone coming to know the Saviour.

One afternoon Amy went straight from school to the hospital. It was spring and they had been making paper daffodils in school. Amy wanted to give hers to Aunt Roberta and she was looking forward to explaining how they had made them.

She knew Aunt Roberta would be interested in that.

'The thing about her,' she thought to herself as she walked down the corridor, 'is that she's not just interested in talking about herself all the time. She listens to other people too.'

As she came close to Aunt Roberta's bed, Amy noticed that today she was lying on the bed, rather than sitting on the chair as she usually did. The 'cross' nurse was standing beside her and they were deep in conversation. Amy could see Aunt Roberta's little, worn Bible lying on the bed-cover. She went and stood by Isobel's bed opposite for a few moments. To her relief, Isobel was sound asleep this afternoon.

When she passed Amy on her way back to her duties, the 'cross' nurse smiled and said, 'That auntie of yours is a lady worth listening to.'

Aunt Roberta seemed tired, but she loved Amy's flowers and asked all about her day. Amy decided not to stay long, but before she left, Aunt Roberta said, 'Amy, there's something I've been meaning to give you. Look in my locker for a small, brown package.'

Amy opened the locker door and was hit by the smell of peppermints mixed with ointment. The locker was, as she might have expected, very tidy and almost empty and she soon found the package. It was an extremely old envelope folded over and over and fastened with a perished elastic band.

'Open it, Amy. I want you to have it and I want to tell you its story.'

Amy undid the package and pulled out a small brooch, obviously silver but very tarnished. There were two linked hearts surrounded by a garland of ivy leaves, but what made Amy gasp was that the word engraved on the hearts was 'MIZPAH'!

'It's a Mizpah brooch,' said Aunt Roberta.

Amy looked blank.

'Perhaps you've never seen one, but they were very fashionable at one time. Lots of young men gave them to their sweethearts if they had to go away. You know why?'

Amy shook her head. 'I know Mizpah means "Watchtower."'

'Ah, but you have to read Genesis 31, the story of Laban parting from Jacob. They built a big pile of stones and gave it the name "Mizpah" or "Watchtower" and Laban said, "The LORD watch between me and thee, when we are absent one from another." I'm not sure that when Laban said those words to Jacob he was being particularly loving, but they sound like tender words and, in my day, if a boy gave a girl a Mizpah brooch he meant, "Let's not forget one another. Let's pray for one another and let's ask God to look after us both all the time we're apart. And let's both live for God when we're apart the way we would if we were together.'"

She paused for a moment and then added, 'At least that's what William meant when he gave me that brooch, but then there were very few as good as William.'

Amy was amazed. Is that what Lisa had meant by her 'MIZPAH' postscript? Something serious and not some joke? But she would have to leave thinking about that till later. She didn't want to miss any of Aunt Roberta's story.

'Who was William?' she asked timidly.

Aunt Roberta's face lit up. 'No one remembers him now, but he was one of the finest young men you could ever hope to meet. We were at Bible College together, but he was a much better Christian than I was. I couldn't believe it when he started to take an interest in me. He gave me that brooch just before I left for Brazil, and I knew then that we would get married some day. He still had a year to study, but after that he was to come to Brazil with my mission. I found Brazil very difficult at first. I missed my mother and father and all my brothers and sisters terribly. It would be six years before I would see them again. And I wasn't really very good at meeting new people or fitting into new situations. God was good and helped me through the hard times, but all the time I was thinking, "Things will soon be better when William comes."'

She stopped again and her faded blue eyes filled with tears. Amy stroked her arm the way she had seen her mother do. The whole story she had imagined around Aunt Roberta was springing back to life. There may not have been a ruby ring, but there had been a handsome young man! But surely William hadn't let Aunt Roberta down?

'What happened?' she whispered.

'William never came. He was killed in an accident. I was devastated. How could I live without William? But God was still there. One of my special verses at that time was Philippians 4:19 "But my God shall supply all your need according to his riches in glory by Christ Jesus." Over the years he did supply whatever I needed—everything. Sometimes he sent me friends to keep me company and encourage me along the way. Sometimes I was alone. He taught me that what I needed more than anything else was Jesus himself. I always liked to have a "watchword" and my new watchword became "Jehovah-jireh."

'"The Lord will provide",' interrupted Amy. She knew the meaning from a song they had learnt at Youth Group.

'The Lord will provide,' repeated Aunt Roberta. Suddenly she seemed very tired, for her eyes closed, and she lay for a while twisting the ring on her thin finger, until Amy was sure she had fallen asleep and tiptoed away.

One evening about two weeks later Amy was already in bed, reading, when she heard the phone ring downstairs. Vaguely she wondered who it was. A few minutes later her bedroom door opened and Mum and Dad came in. She could tell from their faces that they had some bad news and guessed that it had something to do with Aunt Roberta. As gently as they could they told her that she had died peacefully in her sleep that afternoon.

'She's in heaven now,' said Dad. 'That's a far better place for her to be.'

Amy had to agree. When she had been very tired or her arm had been very sore, Aunt Roberta would have sighed and said, 'I think I'd like to go home soon', and Amy had never felt that she had been talking about her shabby, little grey house. Now she would see Jesus. And all her old friends.

And William. She would never be sore or tired again.

When Mum and Dad had gone back downstairs, Amy took the Mizpah brooch out of the drawer in her bedside cabinet. It looked prettier now that she had given it a good polish. She remembered what Aunt Roberta had been like the day she had given it to her—old and frail, but still very much alive. Amy suddenly realized how much she would miss her. She buried her face in her pillow and sobbed until it was quite wet with tears. As she drifted off to sleep, a happier thought popped into her mind. Lisa was sure to come back with her parents for the funeral!

Spring sunshine was streaming through the church windows. Amy had never been to a funeral before and she felt nervous as well as sad. Since Aunt Roberta had outlived most of her friends and family, the congregation was not large, but Amy had noticed the 'cross' nurse sitting in the back row. Lisa came in with her mum and dad! Amy felt excited, but this was neither the time nor the place to show it. Lisa, who had never been so concerned about time or place, gave her a huge grin and a little wave.

Later, in Amy's bedroom, the girls had lots to talk

about. When they came to 'MIZPAH' Lisa seemed rather awkward.

'You see,' she explained, 'I've been finding it hard to be a Christian without you. There are no other Christians in my class in Eldershore and it's difficult. I realized I depended on you a lot.'

'On me?' Amy was surprised.

'I thought we could maybe still help each other. By praying and, well, being there for one another—and things,' she ended a bit lamely. They had never talked like this much before.

'Good idea,' said Amy.

Fortunately Lisa didn't seem jealous when Amy showed her the brooch. 'Imagine Aunt Roberta knowing the MIZPAH idea too!'

She pulled something out of her pocket and handed it to Amy. 'Look what Mum just gave me. Aunt Roberta said I was to have it.'

It was Aunt Roberta's ring. It was old fashioned and heavy and the initials on the front were almost worn away. 'There are some words engraved inside,' she said.

Amy looked. 'Jehova-jireh!' she shrieked. 'It's Aunt Roberta's watchword.'

She told Lisa all about Aunt Roberta's special verse and how God had taught her to depend on him.

Lisa slipped the ring onto her middle finger. 'I think I'll wear this,' she said.

She noticed that Amy had the Mizpah brooch pinned to her sweatshirt.

Just then, Lisa's mum called up the stairs, 'Lisa, we'll have to go now! We've a long journey ahead of us.'

Reluctantly Lisa stood up.

'See you in 115 days,' said Amy, giving her a hug.

Eldershore

Amy hadn't travelled much by train before and certainly never on her own. She was very excited about her visit to Eldershore to see Lisa and only a little worried about the journey, so she hadn't been too pleased when Mum had asked the elderly lady sitting opposite to keep an eye on her and to make sure she got off at Twincastle.

The lady was taking her responsibility very seriously: every time Amy moved she wanted to know if she was all right. Eventually Amy took a book out of her bag and pretended to read. Hopefully that would put an end to all the questions. From the corner of her eye she looked out of the train window. At first everywhere was familiar, even if everything did look a bit different seen from the back. They passed through towns she had been in before, but after an hour or so all the scenery was new, and she felt far from home. In fact, the journey was so long that, towards the end, Amy was glad to put down her book and talk to the inquisitive lady again.

At last they arrived in Twincastle, and there was Lisa waiting on the platform to meet the train. Eldershore was twelve miles away, so the girls had plenty of time to catch up on all the news as they drove there.

'Though I'm not sure how you can have anything new to say to each other,' commented Lisa's mum. 'It's only two weeks since you came back from camp and there have been plenty of letters and phone calls since then.'

Eldershore was not a big place but it was well spread out.

'If you go down there you come to the school,' explained Lisa. 'Our church is along that way, and most of the shops. This is our street now. It leads right down to the sea.'

Amy would hardly have called the road they turned into a 'street'. Although there were houses running down both sides of it, they were so far apart that you must hardly notice your neighbours. Trees lined the road, and the sea sparkled at the bottom of the hill. As they swung in through Lisa's gates, Amy noticed that the strip up the middle of the driveway was grass rather than tarmac, like all the drives of the neat semis at home. And the house was fantastic! It was big and old and rambling and it stood in a garden that was pretty in a wild sort of way.

Lisa's dog, Prince, came bounding out of the

front door to meet them. He was black and tan with one ear that stood up straight and one that flopped over his eye. There was nothing princely about him.

Amy laughed. 'Why did you call him Prince?' she asked.

Lisa shrugged. 'I don't know. I suppose you would have thought up a name and then spent the rest of your life trying to find the right dog to suit it.'

'Probably,' agreed Amy. It was nice to be with Lisa again. They were very different, but they understood each other.

Lisa spent what was left of the afternoon showing Amy round her new home. The tour ended up at Lisa's bedroom window, which had a sea view.

'I can't understand why you don't like Eldershore!' exclaimed Amy. 'I would love to live here. It would be like being on holiday all year round.'

Lisa sat down on her bed. 'It's not that I don't like Eldershore as a place. It's just that it does get a bit lonely. If you want to go to the cinema or bowling you have to go all the way to Twincastle. Or you make a new friend and ask her to come round after school, but that doesn't work either because she lives on a farm ten miles away and goes home on the school bus. There are lots of things I'd like to do, but Mum won't let me go far on my own. It's been better since I got Prince, though, and this week will be fine, because there will be two of us.'

Lisa's mum called them for dinner. By the time they had eaten and Amy had unpacked it was almost bed time, so they had to wait until the next day to explore. They decided to go down to the beach in the morning as it was nice and sunny. Prince went with them. He loved the sea and never seemed to get tired of swimming out to fetch the sticks they threw in for him. The tide was in, but there was still a strip of golden sand running as far as Amy could see. It wasn't anything like the beaches she had been to before where you had to arrive early if you wanted to stake out a square of sand for yourself.

'Where is everyone?' she asked. 'Don't people come to the beach here?'

'Some do, but I told you Eldershore is really out of the way. And the sea is always freezing, even on the hottest day. We'll go swimming one day and you'll see what I mean.'

They carried on along the shore, stopping to look for shells or to skim flat stones across the waves. They took off their shoes and walked along at the water's edge. It certainly was very cold.

'We'd better turn back soon,' said Lisa, 'but I think you'll like the bay around this next corner.'

Like it! Amy thought it was the most beautiful place she had ever seen in her life. An almost perfect crescent of sand was surrounded by low sand dunes. Beyond the dunes the ground began to rise in a gentle grassy slope dotted with trees. A stream gushed down the hillside and cut a channel across the sand on its way to the sea. Looking out across the bay was an old stone house with its garden gate opening straight onto the beach.

'Whoever lives in that house must be the happiest person in the world,' sighed Amy.

'Well, let's go and ask them,' said Lisa and before Amy could object, she had grabbed hold of her arm and was dragging her towards the house. At the gate she had to stop to tie up Prince. Amy wriggled free.

'Lisa, don't be mad. We can't just walk up to some random people's door and ask them if they're the happiest people in the world.'

Lisa laughed loudly. 'Amy, you are such an idiot! Do you think I would do that? I happen to know who lives here. It's Jill from my class. I told you about her in a letter. She comes to church sometimes.'

Amy remembered. She also remembered feeling just a little jealous when she had read that letter.

'Promise you'll not ask her if she's the happiest person in the world,' she begged, still not altogether sure of Lisa's mood.

'No way.' Lisa looked more serious and lowered her voice. 'I don't think she could be. It's all a bit different here. Her dad's not at home and her mum seems to spend most of her life upstairs. You'll like Jill, though. Come on.'

Lisa opened the gate, which seemed to have been made out of driftwood, and they walked up the path to the house. The garden was more like a fenced-off piece of sand dune than a proper garden. It was full of rabbit holes. A toddler was sitting on the front doorstep. He had dark curly hair, lots of freckles and a runny nose.

'Hello, Benjy,' said Lisa. 'Is Jill at home?'

Benjy took one look at the girls, jumped onto his battered trike and headed off round the corner of the house. Lisa knocked on the door, but there was no answer.

'Hi, there, Lisa,' came a voice from behind

them, and they turned round to see a teenage version of Benjy, carrying an enormous basket of washing and a threadbare peg bag.

'Go on in. Jill's in there doing some tidying up.'

'Thanks, Sam,' said Lisa and she opened the door and went in, with Amy following sheepishly behind. They met Jill in the hallway. She had curly hair and freckles like her brothers,. She was wearing a dressing gown much too small for her and she held a tray dangling from one hand.

'Oh, Lisa, it's good to see you. I have something special to tell you. This must be Amy.' She held out her free hand and actually shook hands with Amy.

'Quaint,' thought Amy to herself, but she couldn't help liking Jill straight away.

They went into the living room where Jill started to clear an assortment of glasses and cups off the table.

'A bit dark in here,' she remarked and pulled back the faded green curtains. And there was that marvellous view of the beach and the sea—slightly hazy due to the dirty window panes—but a wonderful view all the same. A black cat jumped up onto the outside sill and Jill opened the window to let him into the room.

'There you go, Hunter,' she said, tickling him under the chin. 'You see what you can catch today.' She turned to Lisa. 'We've just discovered we have mice again. But you'll soon sort them, won't you, Hunter?'

Amy shrank back into her chair. If there was one thing she could not stand it was mice. Her heart was pounding and her arms had come up in goose pimples at the very thought of them. What if one were to run across the floor right now? She would have to get Lisa out of here as soon as possible. But Jill had sat down on the floor beside Lisa and was obviously telling her about the special thing.

'You know my big sister, Kate, who works in London? Well, she's coming home this afternoon. It's my birthday next Thursday and she's going to organize a party for me. Won't you come? And won't Amy still be here? So she can come too.'

Lisa was very excited. Amy tried to be excited too, but all she could think of was mice. Fortunately Lisa soon looked at her watch and realized they would have to go. They untied Prince and set off back along the beach. The tide was starting to go out now.

'Well, did you like Jill?' Lisa wanted to know.

'Yes, I liked her a lot. But, Lisa, I'm sorry, I just can't go to her party.'

Lisa was not one bit understanding about the mice.

'Don't be so silly, Amy. There are mice everywhere round here. Of course there are. It's the country. Don't look so horrified: there are none in our house. You can't refuse to go to Jill's party just because you're scared you might see a mouse. As soon as I arrived here all the girls from the class came up to me one by one to warn me never to go to Jill's house, because it's messy and because her mum's different in some way or other. If you don't go she'll think you're just like them. And I've told her you're a Christian. Get it sorted. Pray about it.'

Amy couldn't remember Lisa ever being that cross with her before. They talked about other things then, and by the time they reached home—half an hour later than they were supposed to be—they were back to normal. Amy didn't bring the subject up with Lisa again, but that night she couldn't sleep for worrying about it. She had chosen to sleep on a folding bed in Lisa's room, so that they wouldn't miss out on any of their time together, but Lisa had already been asleep for hours. The sound of the waves on the shore at the bottom of the hill drifted into the room through the open window. The church clock struck two. Amy turned over in bed again and wondered what she was going to do. One thing was certain: she just couldn't go to the party. She would die if she saw a mouse! 'Pray about it,' Lisa had said. But what was she to pray? That some new disease would wipe out the entire mouse population before Thursday? It was already Sunday morning. Somehow she doubted whether she could ask God to do that for her. Maybe Kate wouldn't come home, or the party would be cancelled for some other reason. But what would Lisa say if she knew that she was praying for that? In the end she made do with, 'Please, God, don't make me have to go to a party where there are mice.' Eventually she fell asleep.

Morning seemed to come very soon, and Amy had to rush to be ready for church in time. She had been looking forward to seeing Lisa's church. It was a large building, but it was nowhere near full. Lisa's family sat near the back, so Amy was able to take a good look at the congregation. Lisa was right: there didn't seem to be many other children there, but then the door opened and in came Jill with Sam, followed by an older girl, who must be Kate, holding a very clean-looking Benjy by the hand. One or two others came in, and the service began. Amy found herself thinking about her church at home. Was everyone wondering where she was when they saw Mum and Dad and Mark there without her? The minister here had an unfamiliar accent. She listened to his voice as he read the Bible passage. It was from 2 Corinthians 12:

... there was given me a thorn in my flesh, a messenger of Satan, to torment me. Three times I pleaded with the Lord to take it away from me. But he said to me, 'My grace is sufficient for you, for my power is made perfect in weakness.'

Then her mind drifted away again. The windows were made up of small panes of coloured glass. She counted how many blue panes there were, then how many yellows and how many greens. Several of the panes had been broken over the years and had been replaced with clear glass. If she moved her head just a little she could see the tops of some trees outside. And could that be the sea? The service came to an end, and everyone went outside. Jill introduced them to Kate and reminded them about the party. Amy smiled, but she didn't want to be reminded. She didn't want it to spoil the rest of her holiday.

And it didn't. The rest of the week was wonderful. They went out in a boat and saw some seals. Lisa's mum took them to a lovely beach with only one other family on it. They swam and afterwards they built a village in the sand and then watched the tide wash it away. They got scratched to bits picking raspberries and then helped make them into jam. One afternoon they went to a village fête and entered Prince in the dog show. He disgraced himself in the 'best-behaved dog' competition, but he won second prize for 'the most comical-looking dog'.

The weather had been good since Amy had arrived, but on Wednesday it poured all day.

'I hope it clears up for Jill's party tomorrow,' said Lisa. 'They're hoping to have a barbecue.'

Amy changed the subject. 'Do you remember when we did this project? We were in Miss Stewart's class.' The girls were spending the afternoon in the garage. The garage had an old hayloft, because long ago it had been the stables for the house. Lisa's mum had stored some boxes there when they had moved to Eldershore, and Amy and Lisa were giggling over some old school books and photographs they had found.

'I need something to eat and drink,' Lisa announced. 'I'll not be a minute.'

She slid down the ladder, and, pulling her sweatshirt up over her head, made a dash through the rain for the house. Left alone, Amy lay back on the old cushions they had brought up to make themselves comfortable and gazed up at the raindrops hammering down on the cobwebby skylight. Looking at all those things from the past had made her feel a bit sad.

Suddenly she heard a little scratching sound and she propped herself up on one elbow to see what it was. A mouse! Her heart started to thump and the goose pimples came up on her arms. If the mouse had scuttled off across the floor and disappeared, Amy would probably have gone on being terrified of mice for the rest of her life, but it didn't: it stopped and looked straight at her. Amy stared back. It was very tiny: it must be a baby. Its eyes were bright and beady, and its coat was brownish-grey. It was nearly the same colour as Mark's rabbit, Smokey, had been, and Amy had liked Smokey a lot. The mouse seemed rooted to the spot, and its little body was quivering.

'He's scared of me,' thought Amy, and to her own surprise, she felt sorry for it.

Just at that moment there was another scuffle, and a bigger mouse ran across the floor. The little one followed it. With two funny little wiggles, they disappeared down a crack.

The garage door burst open and Lisa had arrived, trying to balance two glasses of lemonade and a plate of biscuits on a tray covered with a tea-towel.

'Give me a hand!' she called up to Amy. 'Mum's been baking and the biscuits are still warm. What are you grinning about?'

Amy lifted the glasses off the tray without saying anything, and Lisa didn't wait for an answer. She had remembered that her favourite programme was on TV at four o'clock and she wanted to be tidied up in time to see it.

It rained for the rest of the day and for most of the night, but by Thursday morning the sun was shining again. The girls went in to Twincastle with Lisa's mum who had to go to the supermarket. They chose a T-shirt and a card for Jill's birthday. After lunch they set off along the shore for her party. Prince wasn't with them today so they had time to take a look in the rock pools on the way.

'This is your last day,' said Lisa sadly. 'It's been a really good week. Somehow, I feel more at home in Eldershore with you here. I wish you could live here.'

Amy was quiet. It had been a really good week, but she was starting to miss home now.

The party went well. Kate must have spent the whole week cleaning and tidying. Everyone went into the living room first and Jill opened her presents. She was terribly excited and she loved the T-shirt. Nearly all the girls who had been invited from school had come and today they were all being very nice. Jill's mum was there too, looking far more ordinary than Amy had imagined she would. There were no mice to be seen. After that they all went outside. Kate had organized a treasure hunt on the hill behind the house. Everyone dashed about looking for clues, except for Amy who was last to finish because she got sidetracked into exploring the stream and admiring the views from the hill.

She still thought it was a beautiful place to live.

After the treasure hunt Kate and Sam began to get the barbecue ready, and the girls had a sand sculpture competition on the beach. Benjy wanted to join in too. He was rather clumsy, but he was so cute that no one minded too much. Jill's mum judged the competition and awarded Lisa and Amy first prize for their dolphin.

Kate had bought matching paper cups and napkins for the barbecue. There was plenty to eat and a huge chocolate birthday cake for afterwards. Kate had made that too.

'I wish I had a big sister like yours,' Amy overheard one of the other girls say to Jill.

The sky was pink and gold as Lisa and Amy made their way home.

'Well, did you survive?' asked Lisa.

'Oh, yes, it was a great party.'

'But what about the mice? Did God answer your prayer about that? What did you pray?'

Amy felt her cheeks going red. Wouldn't it have been terrible if the party had been cancelled!

Lisa laughed. 'I can imagine what you prayed. That you wouldn't have to go to the party. That was the wrong prayer. Weren't you listening on Sunday morning? That sermon was meant for you.' A mischievous glint came into her eye. 'In fact, I actually know the minister quite well and I asked him to preach it for you.'

Amy got so flustered that Lisa had to put her out of her misery. 'I'm only joking. I didn't ask him, but I did think it was a good sermon for you.'

Amy admitted that she hadn't really been listening, so Lisa gave her own summary.

'It was about Paul and how there was something wrong with him that was making his life miserable. The Bible calls it 'a thorn in the flesh'. It might have been bad eyesight. Anyway, Paul kept asking God to take it away, but that wasn't God's plan for Paul's life. He wanted to teach Paul to trust him, even when things were really hard. And the lesson for us was that God doesn't always take all the difficulties out of our lives, but that he gives us the strength to live with them.'

'That's exactly how God worked it out for me!' said Amy. 'He helped me not to be scared of mice any more. I never even thought of praying for that.' She told Lisa about the mice in the hayloft.

Lisa stopped walking and drew some patterns in the damp sand with a stick. After a while she looked up, and her face was serious.

'I told you that sermon was for you, but really it was for me too, only I didn't want to listen. You see, I've been asking God for months to change things. First, I wanted him to stop us from coming to Eldershore in the first place. Then I kept praying that Dad's job wouldn't work out and we would have to go back home. Recently I've been praying that your family would come to live here. I suppose I've been getting a bit cross that God hasn't been answering any of these prayers the way I want. Now I think that God isn't going to change the things I don't like. I suppose they must all be part of his plan. Maybe I've been praying the wrong prayer too.'

She threw her stick into the sea, and they both watched it bobbing in the waves for a few moments.

'What do you think is the right prayer?' asked Amy at last.

'That God would help me settle down and be happy here. I think I need to make some proper friends.'

Amy took a deep breath. 'Jill would make a

good friend,' she said.

She thought it would have been nice if Lisa had made a speech about how they would always be best friends, no matter what happened. It would have been exactly the right moment, too, as the sun was just about to sink into the sea. But she knew that wasn't Lisa's style. Still, the friendly slap on the back probably meant the same thing.

'Race you to that big boulder!' shouted Lisa and she sprinted off.

Mince pies

Mrs Morris frowned at the book Holly had handed her. 'Are you sure this is the poem you want to choose? Some of the words in it are very hard.' She paused while she read the poem through. 'In fact, the whole thing's difficult to understand. Why not try something you know already?'

Holly took the book back, but she didn't go and sit down. 'I really, really want to learn this one,' she said. 'I want my mum to hear me saying it. I know she'll like it best, because she likes horses so much.'

Mrs Morris smiled and nodded in what was meant to be an encouraging way. She suspected that Holly had only been attracted to this poem because of the picture of a galloping horse on the opposite page. It was a piece from a Shakespeare play, and it was very difficult. Any of the children would have struggled to learn it. She was beginning to wonder whether her plan for a Christmas concert with everyone in the class taking part was too ambitious. Suddenly she noticed William Aitken causing a disturbance in the corner.

'And you, William, can stop sniggering. I'm not too happy with the poem you've chosen, either. It seems a bit childish—more like something you might have learnt at infant school. In fact, I'm not sure that I don't remember you reciting it when you were in Miss Stewart's class.'

William Aitken looked at her innocently. 'Oh, miss, I really want to choose this one. My mum would love to hear it. She likes teapots so much.'

Sometimes it was impossible to know whether William was trying to be cheeky. Mrs Morris sighed and threw up her hands.

'All right,' she said, 'I'll leave it up to you to choose what to perform at the concert, but it's also up to you to learn it and practise it. We'll start rehearsals next week.'

Not everyone planned to recite a poem. Some of the children had chosen to sing or dance or play their musical instruments. Amy was going to sing a duet with Laura. She felt nervous before the first rehearsal, but Mrs Morris was very positive.

'That was lovely, girls. You both have nice voices. Don't be frightened to sing out louder. Everyone wants to hear you.'

William Aitken had actions for his teapot poem. Mrs Morris had to admit that he was quite entertaining, although she still couldn't decide whether he was trying to be cheeky. Holly stuttered and stumbled her way through the horse poem. Mrs Morris glared at the children who were giggling and hoped Holly might still change her mind. There were, after all, still a few weeks to go.

Amy always loved the weeks leading up to Christmas. There were so many special things happening and so many plans to make. She usually started to think about Christmas shopping near the beginning of November and got frustrated with Mark who left everything till the last minute. Every year the children pooled their pocket money to buy presents for their parents and grandparents, but Mark always seemed to forget that Christmas would come round again in December and usually had no money left.

This year Amy had one extra plan. The idea had started when she had been helping Mum to pack shoeboxes with gifts for children in Eastern Europe who would have no Christmas presents otherwise. Their church had been doing that for years, and Amy really enjoyed thinking of things small enough to fit in. She liked to imagine the children opening the boxes and the happy looks on their faces. It wasn't a big thing, but it was something she could do for Jesus. That had got her wondering whether there was maybe something else she could do for him, something nearer to home. Christmas was such a lovely time for Amy and her family. There must be someone she knew who wouldn't have such a good time and whom she could help just a little.

At last Amy thought of the perfect person—Mrs Smith. Mrs Smith lived at the end of Amy's street. When Amy had been little enough not to feel afraid of adults she didn't know well, but big enough to be allowed to ride her bike up and down the pavement, she had had many chats with Mrs Smith. She had had a very nice front garden and an enormous ginger cat which always seemed to be asleep under the lilac bush. Recently Amy had heard that she was bad with arthritis and hardly got out any more, and that her old cat had died.

'Mum,' announced Amy one afternoon as soon as she came in the back door from school, 'I'm going to bake some mince pies and take them to Mrs Smith.'

'That's a lovely idea,' said Mum. 'Would you like some help?'

'No, thanks. I can manage.'

Amy wanted this to be her very own project and she couldn't wait to get started. They had made pastry in school one day, and she had written the recipe down in a notebook, so she washed her hands, gathered her ingredients together and set to work. But nothing seemed to go right. First of all she spilled the flour and had to spend ten minutes clearing it up. Then the dough was far too crumbly and broke into a thousand pieces when she tried to roll it out.

'Try adding a little more water,' suggested Mum.

'Now it's too sticky,' wailed Amy a few moments later, but she persevered and eventually had twelve rather grey-looking circles of pastry lying on the work surface—six for the bases of the pies and six for the lids.

Mum was getting the evening meal ready. 'Don't put too much mincemeat in,' she advised. Amy made a hole in the top of each pie and sprinkled some sugar on the top. Mum popped them in the oven. 'You'd better tidy up and then start your homework,' she said. 'I'll take your pies out when they're ready.'

Mark was late coming home. He had been at rugby training. 'What's that burning smell?' he asked as he came into the kitchen.

'Amy's been baking mince pies and some of the filling has leaked out and burnt in the oven. But the pies aren't burnt,' said Mum cheerily.

'Are those the pies?' asked Mark. 'I hope she's not expecting us to eat them.'

'No, she made them especially for old Mrs Smith down the road. It's a really kind idea and she tried her very best, so don't tease her about them.'

Amy was disappointed with the pies when she saw them herself, but the next afternoon Mum found her a little basket to put them in, and by the time she had arranged them on some red tissue paper and sprinkled some more sugar on the top, they didn't look too bad. Now for the difficult part! It was a long time since she had spoken to the old lady. Slowly she set off along the street. Mrs Smith's garden gate was open, and a huge pile of dead leaves had gathered behind it. The hedge, which had always been so neatly trimmed, was overgrown, and the lilac bush was almost smothered in ivy. Balancing the precious basket in one hand, Amy reached up to ring the doorbell. She couldn't help noticing that the paint was beginning to flake off the door and that the lace curtains at the windows were grubby. The doorbell definitely worked. Amy had heard it echoing in the hallway, but it was so long before anyone answered the door that she had almost decided that Mrs Smith didn't live there any more. When at last she did come, Amy got a shock. Mrs Smith had been tall and stately; now she looked small and hunched. She had always been neat and tidy; now her hair was uncombed and she was wearing a dirty cardigan. Her face had been smiley; now she looked worried.

Amy took a deep breath. 'Hello, Mrs Smith, I'm Amy,' she began bravely.

Mrs Smith's expression did not change. Amy tried again. 'I live along the street. I used to visit you when I was little. I've made you some mince pies for Christmas.' She held out the basket.

Mrs Smith looked at the pies and poked one with her finger. She shook her head. 'No thank you, dear,' she said and closed the door.

For a few seconds Amy stood with her mouth wide open, then, with the pies clutched to her chest, she ran all the way home, tears pouring down her cheeks. Mum sat her down at the kitchen table and tried to reason with her.

'Mrs Smith probably didn't know who you were. You've grown up a lot. And sometimes when people get older they get confused. I'm sure she wouldn't have meant to hurt you. Your idea was a lovely one. You did it for Jesus and he's pleased with you, even if it didn't work out how you meant it to. Remember the story about the widow who put all the money she had into the offering plate. It was very little, but Jesus knew her heart was right and he praised her. Dad will be more than happy to eat your pies.'

Amy looked at the pies, which were now very battered. 'They're horrible, and it was all just a waste of time,' she said. It would certainly be a very long time before she would try anything like that again!

The class concert was to take place that Friday afternoon. Mrs Morris came to school in the morning looking especially smart in high-heeled shoes and a frilly blouse, but by lunchtime she was hot and bothered.

'William Aitken, if I have to speak to you one more time, you will not be performing this afternoon,' she warned, before turning to Holly. 'Holly, you still don't know that poem off by heart.' Suddenly she had an idea. 'Amy, you're the first on. When you've finished you can come and stand here in the wings, just behind the curtain. I'll give you a copy of Holly's poem and then if she gets stuck you can whisper the words to her. That's known as "prompting". Isn't that a good idea?' Both girls nodded, and the final rehearsal continued.

At last the afternoon arrived, and there was a hum of excited voices where the children had gathered behind the stage. William had sneaked out into the corridor from where he could see the main door of the school and was giving a running commentary as the parents arrived. Amy's tummy felt funny. It wasn't so much like butterflies, more like a whole basketful of kittens wriggling around in there.

The children had practised on the stage several times before, but the hall had always been empty then. Now it was packed full of parents and friends, looking a little uncomfortable in their outdoor coats, perched on the child-sized chairs. Amy felt her legs trembling as she and Laura walked onto the stage, but once they started singing her nerves disappeared, and they sang as well as they ever had before.

'Well done,' said Mrs Morris as they came back behind the curtain, and the girls smiled and glowed with pride.

Amy took up her position in the wings and looked at the book with Holly's poem in it. 'Help!' she thought. 'I hope she doesn't get stuck. I can't read half these words myself.'

From where she was standing Amy could see the audience as well as the performers. It was William's turn. He was saying his teapot poem with great enthusiasm. Amy was able to pick out his mum in the crowd. Yes, she seemed to be enjoying his performance. So did everyone else. There was her own mum, sitting beside Laura's, laughing and clapping loudly.

Holly was on next. Amy felt the kittens tumbling around in her tummy again, but Holly walked confidently onto the stage. She smiled down at her mum, who was sitting in the very front row, and started loud and clear: 'I will not change my horse with any that treads.'

It was a good start, but Holly soon lost her way and several times she glanced across to Amy for help. Amy whispered the forgotten words and felt flustered. She glanced from the poetry book to Holly, then to Holly's mum. The poem seemed to be lasting forever, although it was really quite short. Holly was completely focused on what she was doing and did not appear to be at all flustered. Her mum was sitting on the edge of her seat, smiling encouragingly the whole time.

'Nearly there,' thought Amy.

'… His countenance enforces homage,' finished Holly.

For a moment there was silence. No one was sure that that was the end. The silence was broken by a loud cheer. Holly's mum was on her feet applauding wildly. The rest of the parents clapped politely too.

'How embarrassing,' thought Amy, but Holly was beaming from ear to ear.

'I knew she'd like it,' she whispered to Amy as she left the stage.

Amy peeped at Holly's mum from behind the curtain. She appeared to be wiping a tear from the corner of her eye. 'She doesn't care what Holly performed like. She's just so pleased that she chose a poem especially for her and put in all that effort,' thought Amy. Was that how parents felt? Maybe that really was how God felt about the mince pie episode.

'Amy, you're day-dreaming again,' said Mrs Morris. 'Our guests are waiting.'

The class was to serve tea to the parents and friends after the concert. They had set up tables at the back of the hall and had been busy making table decorations and baking shortbread. Amy was to be a milk-pourer. She hurried to take up her place behind the table beside Laura. As the grown-ups filed past to collect their tea they congratulated the children. Amy noticed her mother approaching with Miss Anderson. Miss Anderson was a smartly dressed lady who went to their church. She always seemed to be busy organizing things. Amy liked her, but she was a little afraid of her. At first she couldn't think why she was at the concert, but then she remembered that she was on the school's board of governors.

'Amy, dear,' said Miss Anderson, as she held out her tea cup for some milk. 'You and you friend here have a wonderful talent. I had no idea you could sing so well. But now that I do know, I have just the way for you to use your voices to bring pleasure to others.'

She explained that she was in charge of organizing a little concert at Goldenglades, a local home for the elderly, and that she was looking for people to take part.

'You will come on Saturday 20th, won't you, girls? It means so much for the old people to see some young ones.'

Laura agreed rather reluctantly. It was difficult to turn down Miss Anderson. Amy was more enthusiastic. She still wanted to find some way to show Jesus' love to others. This might work out: she could sing better than she could bake.

The matron came forward to greet the girls as they stepped into the foyer of Goldenglades that Saturday afternoon. She looked kind, but efficient.

'It's nice of you to come,' she said. 'Children remind the old folk of their own childhood and that makes them happy. Now, have either of you had much experience of the elderly?'

Laura shook her head. Her own grandparents were young. Amy told about visiting Aunt Roberta.

'And did Aunt Roberta ever become muddled?' asked the matron.

'Hardly ever,' answered Amy.

'Well, I think I'd better warn you girls that some of our residents can be confused. Some of them suffer from what we call "short-term memory loss". That means that they can remember things that happened years ago, but they can't remember what they said or did just a few moments ago. Some of them don't even know their own families, which is very sad. So don't be surprised if they ask you the same question several times. Now, we'll go and find Miss Anderson.'

Miss Anderson was busy arranging things in the lounge. She had set up a microphone on a stand in the middle of the floor, and the sofas and armchairs were arranged in a semi-circle around it. Care assistants were leading the residents to the seats. Laura and Amy sat down awkwardly on the edge of a sofa and smiled stiffly at a shy young man who was obviously going to play his violin.

'How did you get me into this?' whispered Laura. 'This place is strange. It looks like a hotel, but it doesn't feel like one.'

Amy wasn't listening. She was staring at one of the old ladies who had been helped into the room, and wondering whether it could possibly be Mrs Smith. If it was, she had had her hair permed and someone had bought her a nice blue twinset since Amy had seen her two weeks ago. Miss Anderson came over to talk to the girls about what they were going to sing, but Amy kept watching the old lady out of the corner of her eye. She seemed unable to decide where to sit and moved from seat to seat before settling down behind Amy and Laura.

Miss Anderson had just stood up to make her welcoming speech when Amy heard a panic-stricken voice behind her complaining, 'I've lost my handbag.' She turned round to see Mrs Smith—she was sure now that it was Mrs Smith—searching all around her seat. Miss Anderson stopped speaking while everyone looked for the missing handbag. Amy was the one to find it. She remembered where Mrs Smith had been sitting before she moved. Mrs Smith gave her a beautiful smile. 'You are such a good girl,' she said.

The concert began. Miss Anderson herself said a long poem. Some of the old people seemed to know it and joined in at places. The shy young man played his violin. 'Very squeaky,' remarked someone in a loud voice when he had finished, and Amy hoped he hadn't heard, but he went so red that she guessed he had. Then it was the girls' turn to sing. They didn't sing nearly as well as they had done at the school concert. 'There was something funny about that microphone,' complained Laura. The old people seemed to enjoy it, anyway. Next the matron played the piano and everyone sang some old songs together. Laura and Amy didn't know the songs. They looked at one another and tried not to giggle.

'Stay for tea,' said Matron when the singing was finished.

'I'm sorry,' said Laura quickly. 'I have to go shopping in town.'

Amy stayed and helped to pass round the sandwiches. Mrs Smith refused to have anything to eat or drink. She had been fidgety throughout the concert even though one of the care assistants had sat with her the whole time. Now she was sitting all alone looking worried. Amy sidled up to her and sat down gingerly on the chair beside her.

'Hello, Mrs Smith,' she began.

'Hello, dear. I've lost my handbag.'

Amy bent down and lifted the handbag onto Mrs Smith's lap.

The old lady smiled again. 'Thank you so much. You're a good girl. What's your name?'

'I'm Amy. I used to live near you. When I was younger I used to visit you. You always gave me a lollipop and told me stories about when you were a little girl.'

'Is that so, dear? I knew you were a good girl. What's your name?'

Amy told her again and wondered what else she could talk about. 'I used to like your cat.'

'My cat? Yes, I miss my cat. What was he called?'

Amy thought for a moment. 'James,' she remembered.

Mrs Smith started to talk about James and the funny things he had done over the years. She sounded happy. 'That's the way she used to tell me stories years ago,' thought Amy.

Suddenly Mrs Smith's voice changed, and an anxious look came over her face. 'Have you seen my handbag?' she asked.

Patiently Amy patted the handbag, which was still sitting on her lap.

Mrs Smith was reassured. 'Thank you. You're a good girl. What's your name?'

'I'm Amy.'

'Ah, yes, Amy. Did I ask you that before?'

Amy just smiled, and then Matron came along and sat down beside them. 'Are you having a nice chat with Amy, Mrs Smith?' she asked.

'Amy is an old friend of mine,' answered Mrs Smith.

'Well, isn't that nice?' said Matron in a comforting voice and was surprised when Amy explained that it was actually true.

'We've been talking about James,' continued Mrs Smith.

'You often talk about James, don't you, Mrs Smith?' said Matron and she turned to Amy. 'Do you know who James is?'

She smiled when she heard that James was a cat. All the staff had been trying to work out who he could be since Mrs Smith had arrived at Goldenglades the week before.

'Amy,' said Matron thoughtfully. 'I'd like to have a little chat with you.'

Amy said goodbye to Mrs Smith and followed Matron out to the foyer.

'I've been watching you talking to Mrs Smith,' began Matron. 'She was having a proper conversation with you and she was smiling. That's the first time I've seen that since she arrived here. I think that somewhere deep inside she remembers you. What's more, you know some things about her past, either from knowing her yourself or because she's told you stories from her earlier years. Mrs Smith is in an unusual position because both her sons live in Australia and it may be months before they can come home to see her. So far she's had no other visitors. I expect all her own friends are elderly too. Do you think you could pop in and have a chat with her now and again? It would really help her.'

'Poor Mrs Smith,' thought Amy. 'Yes, I'll come,' she promised.

Miss Anderson gave Amy a lift home.

'Well,' she said, 'I feel so encouraged by this afternoon.'

Amy looked at her in surprise. The concert hadn't exactly been a runaway success.

'God has a wonderful way of working things out,' Miss Anderson went on. 'When I heard you and Laura sing at the school I decided to invite you to come and perform at Goldenglades, but I was unsure about asking you. Some girls and boys are terrified of old people. Then your mum told me how good you had been at visiting Aunt Roberta. And now it turns out that you are the one person who knows something about the mysterious Mrs Smith. God has given you a lovely gift, Amy, and he has provided you with a wonderful opportunity to use it. Giving some of yourself and your time to Mrs Smith will make a big difference to the quality of her life.'

'I suppose I quite like chatting to old people,' said Amy shyly. She had never thought of that as anything special before, but she was excited to think that God had given her a task to do for him.

'Mind you,' added Miss Anderson, 'it's not an easy thing to do. Mrs Smith might not always know who you are or thank you for coming. When you feel discouraged remember you're doing it for Jesus.'

A vivid picture of Holly's mother at the school concert flashed across Amy's mind.

'I will,' she said.

Mystery at Ardfuar

D ad put down his cup and looked at Amy, who was still wearing her pyjamas and dawdling over her toast. 'Have you decided whether you're coming with us?' he asked.

Amy looked out of the window at the grey clouds scudding across the sky and then back at the nice warm kitchen. 'I don't know. What are you going to be doing, Mum?'

'I'm going to light a fire and spend a lovely cosy day doing cross stitch. I don't think a cold day at Easter in the north of Scotland is the right time or place for me to start cycling again.'

Amy had made up her mind. A day trying to keep up with Dad and Mark on the bikes would certainly be better than a day alone with Mum if she was working on her cross stitch. 'I'll come,' she said, 'but you mustn't cycle too fast.'

'And you mustn't cycle too slow,' said Mark. He was already dressed and itching to get going. There was a ruined castle in the area he was especially eager to see.

Half an hour later Mark opened the front door of the cottage and called up the stairs. The three bikes were lined up against the garden wall, and he had already stowed the food, the drinks and the raincoats away in the saddlebags. He couldn't wait much longer! Amy came bounding down the stairs, but she had forgotten her hat and had to run back up again. Then Dad came out of the kitchen with the Bible in his hand and ushered them in for their daily reading. This morning it was Psalm 139. Mark found it hard to concentrate, but Amy listened carefully. It was amazing! God knew everything about every single person, right down to when they stood up and sat down. No one could ever have a single thought that God didn't know about, or go anywhere without God being there too.

At last they were off! Mum stood at the cottage gate and waved until they had turned round the first bend. The morning had brightened up. There was still a cold breeze blowing, but the clouds were white now instead of grey, and the sky in-between was blue. The plan was to cycle towards the sea and then follow the coast road to the castle, which was perched on top of a cliff. Mark had planned the route. He was cycling at a reasonable speed, and Amy had time to look around her at the lambs on the hillside and at the stunted trees buckled over by the winds.

When they reached the coast everyone stopped to admire the view. Near the shore the sea was heaving and tossing, and breaking in foamy waves against the steep cliffs. Further out the dark, ruffled water stretched on and on until it met the horizon. Amy watched the gulls as they dipped and soared above the sea and then disappeared into the distance. She had a drink, and then they set off again. This road was all uphill, and Amy soon felt her legs getting tired. She would have liked to get off and push, but she knew that would only make Mark cross, so she struggled on. At least the wind was behind them.

About a mile further on Dad stopped and waited for her to catch up. 'Are you OK?' he asked. Amy was too breathless to answer. 'Just a little further. We're going to stop at Ardfuar for lunch.'

Bravely Amy remounted. 'How can you be cold and hot at the same time?' she wondered. Her fingers and nose were freezing, but her body was warm with all the effort she was making. '"Just a little further",' she snorted after a while. 'Where is this Ardfuar place? I really can't go on.' A few tears of exhaustion and frustration trickled down her cold cheek. In the end she had to push her bike up an especially steep hill. Round the next bend she was relieved to see Dad and Mark waiting for her beside a gate on the sea side of the road.

'You made it,' said Mark. 'This is Ardfuar.' He led the way along a track to a grassy headland high above the sea.

Amy threw her bike onto the grass, flopped down beside it and looked around her. The headland was dotted with ruined, stone cottages. It seemed to be the remains of a village. Mark had read about it in a guidebook. 'They built this village for the people who were cleared off the land when the landowners wanted to make way for their sheep. The men fished for herring from the harbour below the cliff, and the women had to carry the full creels up 236 steps. The book says the steps are still there.'

He wanted to have a look, but Dad said that the slope was far too steep, and the grass too slippery with last night's rain.

'The villagers had to tie up their children like animals in case they slipped or were blown into the sea,' Mark informed them.

'I can well believe it,' said Dad. 'Now, what about something to eat?'

As soon as lunch was over Mark was ready to set

off for the castle. Amy was not. She had seen how the road climbed higher and higher and she knew she would never make it. 'Let me wait here,' she begged.

Dad was torn in two. He knew how much Mark wanted to see the castle and he couldn't let him go alone, but was it safe to leave Amy here? 'All right,' he said at last. 'I know I can trust you, Amy. Wait for us here. Don't go beyond the last cottage. Promise.'

Amy promised. After they had gone she wandered among the ruined cottages, imagining them with thatched roofs and peat smoke coming out of the chimneys and tethered children playing in front of them. The last cottage, the one nearest the sea, was bigger than the others. It was also less tumbledown and had the remains of a slate roof. Amy went to have a closer look. That was strange! There was a bicycle leaning against the wall. It was an old-fashioned, upright bike, but it wasn't rusty. In fact, it looked as if someone had put it there today. Amy's heart missed a beat. Was there someone here? A completely deserted village seemed quite safe. A deserted village with just one other person in it was terrifying!

'What do you think you're doing here? Don't

you know you're trespassing?'

Amy's heart missed two beats. She swung round to face an angry-looking woman. It would have been hard to say what age she was. Her long, dark hair had only a few streaks of grey. Her face was weather-beaten and leathery, but her cheeks were rosy and her blue eyes were very bright. She wore several layers of clothes and a pair of men's boots.

'I—I'm sorry,' stammered Amy and took a couple of steps backwards.

'Don't you know who this village belongs to?'

Amy shook her head.

'It belongs to us. The Murrays. Don't let anyone tell you otherwise. Wasn't my father the last man to live in Ardfuar? In this very house.'

The strange woman gently stroked one of the stones in the wall of the old house as if it was a favourite pet, and went on.

'I was born here, you know? In 1950. The last of fifteen children.'

Amy forgot to be so scared and began to be interested. 'Fifteen children! Were there any twins or triplets?'

'No, no twins or triplets. Just one after the other. "Steps and stairs," my father said. He was a good man, my father. Alexander Murray, a good man. No one could say otherwise. And my mother, Anna, she was a good woman, too. Think of the work she had looking after fifteen children on the edge of a cliff! My father built that wall round our cottage to keep his children from being swept into the sea. With his own hands he carried every stone from the ruins of the other cottages. Oh, yes, we Murrays were here long after everyone else had deserted Ardfuar. And what thanks did we get? When my father was an old, frail widower they told him he couldn't live here any more and they carted him off to some modern house in town. He didn't last long there, I can tell you. Now where is the justice in that?'

The woman was becoming angry again. Her eyes flashed at Amy. 'And now people come wandering about here as if Ardfuar belonged to them. Well, it doesn't. It belongs to me, Ina Murray. Who's the only one who comes back to the old home? Who's the only one who remembers all the birthdays and death-days? Ina Murray! Who does it belong to?'

'To Ina Murray,' repeated Amy.

'Be off with you, then, or I'll call the police,' screamed Ina Murray and she waved her arms around.

If Amy had been thinking straight she might have wondered how Ina Murray was going to carry out her threat. There was no other human being in sight, and the nearest police station was probably miles away, but Amy did not stop to reason that through. She ran back to the gate, seized her bike and cycled off in the direction they had come. It was downhill this time, and she quickly gathered speed, so that she had covered some distance before she realized what she had done. She had promised Dad that she would not move from Ardfuar and she had broken that promise! What else should she have done? And what should she do now?

She pulled on her brakes and, just as she slowed down, she noticed a road leading off to her left. She would turn in here, wait a few minutes and then start back up the hill. By that time Dad and Mark should have returned from the castle and she could explain what had happened. She hoped Dad would understand.

This road was narrow. It was sheltered from the wind by thick gorse bushes on either side and it was pleasantly flat. Amy wondered where it led. She thought she must be nearly at the edge of the cliff by now. Suddenly she arrived at a stone wall with a rusty iron gate in it. Amy pushed open the gate and stepped into a small graveyard. The headstones were not lined up in rows, but looked as if they had sprouted out of the ground where they pleased. Many of them were bent over like the trees she had seen earlier. Part of the far wall had slipped down the cliff into the sea, and sheep had cropped the grass short. Amy walked among the graves and tried to read some of the inscriptions on the headstones. She stopped beside one. The name was worn away, but, after she had cleared away some lichen, she could read most of a rhyme inscribed below:

..................................near,
For here I lie till Christ appear,
And by his grace I hope to have
A joyful rising from the grave.

Another stone just opposite caught her eye. The surname 'Murray' was inscribed in large letters across the top. 'Any relation of my friend Ina Murray?' she wondered and stooped down to have a look. What she read made her gasp:

MURRAY

In loving memory
of
Alexina Murray
1950–1973

How weird to find the grave of someone with the same name and born in the same year as the woman she had just met! 'Don't be silly, Amy,' she told herself. 'Murray's probably a common name round here. It's just a coincidence.' But what came next was even more puzzling:

And of her mother
Anna Murray
1907–1982

And of her father
Alexander Murray
(Last resident of Ardfuar)
1896–1983

This was Ina Murray's grave! All the names were right. Everything fitted in with what the woman at Ardfuar had told her. So who was the strange woman and why was she pretending to be someone who had died years ago? Storylines from adventure books began to flash through Amy's mind. Maybe 'Ina' knew of treasure hidden beneath the Murray cottage. Maybe she was a wanted criminal hiding from the law. Maybe she had lost her memory and didn't know who she was. Amy shivered. Suddenly she felt cold and lonely, and suddenly she remembered that she had stayed here far longer than she had intended.

It was hard work cycling back up the hill. The sky had clouded over again and it had begun to rain. Amy hoped Dad and Mark would be at the gate waiting for her and she began to work out how she would explain everything to them. But there was no one there. Amy left her bike against the fence and went searching among the cottages. She was afraid to call out in case 'Ina Murray' was still about. Quietly she tiptoed up to the last house to see if the old bike was still propped against the wall. It wasn't, but in its place was a modern one.

'Mark!' shrieked Amy, and Mark appeared round the corner of the house. He was very relieved to see Amy, and, as people often do when they are relieved to see someone they have been worried about, he shouted at her.

'Amy, where have you been? We thought you had fallen over the edge of the cliff. Dad is furious with you.'

This was not the welcome Amy had been hoping for, and she shouted back.

'I'd like to know what you would have done if you met a dangerous impostor who threatened to hand you over to the police!'

Mark laughed. He was about to tell Amy to stop talking rubbish, but then he noticed that she really was distressed and that she was getting very wet standing outside in the rain.

'Come and shelter in here and let's hear your story,' he said. 'Dad's gone to see if he could find you and he told me to wait here in case you came back.'

The last cottage still had four walls and part of a slate roof. Beneath the good part of the roof someone had knocked some old planks of wood together to divide off a sort of room. There was a rough door in the makeshift wall, and Mark pushed it open. Amy glanced a round the room. It was quite gloomy, although there was some light filtering in through a small window, which still had all its panes. The original fireplace was still there too, and it looked as if a fire had been burning in the grate very recently. A battered old kettle and a few cups were lying around, and in the corner was an ancient armchair heaped with some ragged blankets and cushions. There was a damp, musty smell and streaks on the walls where water had come through, but it was certainly a wonderful place to shelter.

'Close the door and come on in,' said Mark.

Amy hung back. 'What if Ina Murray lives here?'

'Someone might come here from time to time, but nobody lives here,' said Mark impatiently. 'Who on earth is Ina Murray anyway?'

Amy sat down on the arm of the ancient armchair and told Mark the whole story.

'You do meet some of the most unusual people,' he said when she had finished. 'I'm sure there's some perfectly ordinary explanation,' he added in a big-brotherly voice, but he found himself hoping that this Ina Murray would not decide to come back to Ardfuar that afternoon.

Amy peered out of the window. 'There seems to be a storm brewing up,' she said. Rain was falling heavily and the wind was driving it against the window panes. She could hear the waves crashing far below, but it was now late afternoon and she could no longer see the sea. A lighthouse on some distant headland winked regularly and reassuringly through the gathering darkness.

Mark was rummaging around in a rickety cupboard fastened to the wall. 'I've found a candle and some matches,' he announced. 'There are some dry sticks here. I'm going to light a fire.'

'Do you think we should? Mum's always told us about not playing with fire.'

'That was years ago. I think I'm old enough now. Anyway, you're hardly the one to lecture anyone on keeping the rules.'

Amy wrapped a rug round herself and curled up on the armchair. She felt miserable. She knew she ought not to have disobeyed, but she wished Mark would try to understand how the whole thing had happened. Would Dad understand?

'God knows exactly what you were thinking.' The thought seemed to pop into her mind from nowhere. Then she remembered that morning's Bible reading. 'Mark,' she said. 'Can you remember the psalm we read this morning?'

Mark stuck the candle into the neck of a milk bottle and lit it. It gave a comforting glow. 'No,' he admitted. 'But there's a Bible in this cupboard.'

'Really?' Amy was surprised.

Mark handed her an enormous old Bible wrapped up in an oilskin tablecloth. It smelt funny and the pages were crinkled with damp, but the print was huge, so Amy had no trouble reading the psalm by candlelight. She felt a lot happier once she had finished. God knew that she and Mark were sitting on the edge of a dark cliff in the middle of a storm, but light and darkness were all the same to him. He knew all her thoughts and actions—why she had left Ardfuar, how she hadn't come back straight away. He knew where Dad was now and when he would come. He knew exactly who 'Ina Murray' was. He even knew the nameless person waiting for the resurrection day in the graveyard at the foot of the hill. Amy drifted slowly off to sleep.

She was rudely awakened by a triumphant cry of 'Solved!' Mark was kneeling in front of a bright little fire, clutching the large Bible in both hands. Amy slipped down onto the floor beside him and peered at the front page. It was covered in faded copperplate writing.

'Look, this is the Murrays' old family Bible and all the births, deaths and marriages are recorded on this page. I've found all fifteen children, including your Ina. Only you assumed she was Alexina, but she's not: she's Wilhelmina.'

'But "Ina Murray" told me she was born in 1950 and the Alexina in the graveyard was born in 1950. And I know there were no twins.'

'Alexina and Wilhelmina were both born in 1950, but they weren't twins.' He pointed to the bottom of the page:

Alexina, born 11th January, 1950. Died 6th April 1973.
Wilhelmina, born 23rd December, 1950.

'I never thought of that. So Ina Murray isn't an impostor after all.'

'No,' grinned Mark.

For a while they sat in silence.

'The storm's really wild now,' said Amy. 'When do you think Dad will come?'

'Oh, soon,' said Mark vaguely.

Suddenly there was a sound at the door. Amy jumped up. 'Dad,' she said eagerly. But it was not Dad who came through the door, but a much bigger man, wearing a very wet overcoat, a cloth cap and wellington boots.

'Hello, who have we here?' he asked in

surprise.

While Mark was explaining how they came to be there, a woman in a headscarf struggled into the room. 'Is she there, Donald?' she said anxiously.

Of course she was surprised too, and Mark had to tell his story all over again.

'Well,' said the woman, sitting down in the armchair, 'this is a remarkable night for lost people. I'm Alice Murray and this is my husband, Donald. We're looking for Donald's sister, Ina. She often comes here. She's not at home and we came here to look first. To tell the truth, we're very worried about her. It's such a bad night and it's past the time for her to take her tablets. And she needs them.'

Amy told the Murrays about meeting Ina earlier in the day.

'I hope she wasn't shouting at you,' said Mr Murray. 'She really believes Ardfuar belongs to her. But where did she go after that?'

No one spoke for a few minutes. Suddenly Amy jumped to her feet. 'Let me see the Bible again. I think Ina will be at the graveyard. She told me she remembered all the birthdays and death-days of her family and this is 6th April, the day Alexina died.'

Mrs Murray threw her arms around Amy. 'You are such a clever girl. We should have thought of that. We'll go straight there now. Do you want to come and then we can take you home?'

'No,' said Amy, 'we mustn't move from here, but maybe you could go to the cottage and tell Mum and Dad we're still here.'

As it turned out, that wasn't necessary. Mum and Dad drove into Ardfuar as the Murrays were driving out. There was a very happy reunion in the funny little room. Amy was anxious to explain everything. 'You see, I didn't mean to disobey. I was afraid of trespassing, and I was scared of Ina Murray. And then, by the time I remembered, I was at the bottom of the hill. And I did spend too long in the graveyard and I'm sorry about that ...'

Dad wanted to know who Ina Murray was, but Mark interrupted. 'Let's go home. I'm starving. It's one of Amy's adventures—really complicated. She can tell you in the car.'

The journey home was slow because of the bad weather. After Amy had told her story Dad told his.

'We didn't stay long at the castle because there wasn't much to see there, and because I was worried about leaving you alone at Ardfuar. I shouldn't have let you out of my sight. And then you had gone! I left Mark behind and searched everywhere for you. All the time I was praying, "I don't know where Amy is, but you do, Lord. Look after her." And he did. Then the weather turned bad and I decided to go back to the cottage and get the car. But the road was flooded because of all the heavy rain. We had to take a detour and we got lost. That's why it took us so long to get back.'

The storm had more or less blown itself out by the next day, but the whole family felt tired and spent a lazy day at the cottage. Mr and Mrs Murray called to deliver Mark and Amy's bikes which they had rescued from Ardfuar, and to thank Amy for her help. They had found Ina at Alexina's grave, soaked to the skin. She was with them, too. She greeted Amy like a long-lost friend and admired Mum's cross stitch. Apparently she was quite an expert herself.

A couple of weeks after the holiday Mark handed Amy a photograph. 'I thought you might like this. I took it that afternoon when I was waiting for you.'

It was a magnificent shot of Ardfuar. Ina

Murray's cottage was in the foreground and beyond were the cliffs and the sea and the sky. A seagull hovered above the water. Amy framed it and hung it on her wall. Underneath the picture she had printed some words from Psalm 139:

If I rise on the wings of the dawn,
    if I settle on the far side of the sea,
even there your hand will guide me,
    your right hand will hold me fast.

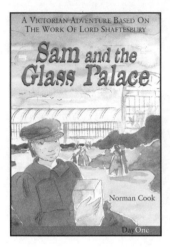

SAM AND THE GLASS PALACE

A VICTORIAN ADVENTURE BASED ON THE WORK OF LORD SHAFTESBURY

NORMAN COOK
PAPERBACK, 96PP, £4
ISBN 1 903087 42 8,
REF SAM 428

Sam Clarke is an orphan, forced to run the streets, who dearly wants an education but, above all, who needs a new mum and dad to take care of him. After coming into contact with Lord Shaftesbury and the Ragged School Union, the first part of his dream starts to come true. But will the dream turn to a nightmare when Sam's wicked uncle, Pineapple Jack, suddenly appears, or will the young shoeblack win through with the help of his friends?

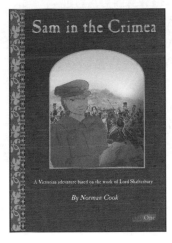

SAM IN THE CRIMEA

A VICTORIAN ADVENTURE BASED ON THE CRIMEAN WAR

NORMAN COOK PAPERBACK, 96PP, £5, ISBN 978 1 84625 045 3, REF SAMC 453

Join Sam Clarke and Carrots the donkey as they hide on board a ship bound for the Crimea... Follow them through the streets of Constantinople, where Sam and his new gypsy friends take on cut-throats and bandits. Lie low in the 'Valley of Death' as they witness the Charge of the Light Brigade and encounter Florence Nightingale. This sequel to *Sam and the Glass Palace* keeps you reading right to the end!

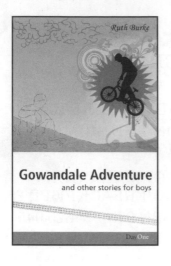

GOWANDALE ADVENTURE
AND OTHER STORIES
FOR BOYS

RUTH BURKE
PAPERBACK,96PP, £5
ISBN 978-1-84625-070-5

It's hard being a Christian, and trying to live for God among our friends. Mark is a normal boy who, like us, doesn't always find it easy to understand and put into practice what God says in the Bible. In these five stories, Mark finds himself in danger at times; he also discovers that it takes courage to stand up for God, and that we often fail to obey him as we should.

Enjoy these exciting adventures with Mark and his friends, and learn with him the lessons God teaches him about following him and living according to the Bible.